Moonbow

Moonbow
An Ode to the Sacred Cosmic Dimensions of
Earth, Spirit, Love and Life

Jessika Le Corre

Sunstone books may be purchased for educational, business,
or sales promotional use.

For information please write:
Special Markets Department, Sunstone Press,
P.O. Box 2321, Santa Fe, New Mexico 87504-2321.
Printed on acid-free paper

Library of Congress Cataloging-in-Publication Data

Names: Le Corre, Jessika, 1981- author.
Title: Moonbow : an Ode to the Sacred cosmic dimensions of Earth, Spirit,
Love and Life / by Jessika Le Corre.
Description: Santa Fe, N.M. : Published by Sunstone Press, [2018]
Identifiers: LCCN 2018015656 | ISBN 9781632932297 (hardcover : alk. paper)
Classification: LCC PS3612.E2125 A6 2018 | DDC 811/.6--dc23
LC record available at https://lccn.loc.gov/2018015656

Moonbow photography by Erik Tranberg Erwan Le Corre
And Jessika Le Corre

SUNSTONE PRESS
Post Office Box 2321, Santa Fe, NM 87504-2321
(505) 988-4418 / orders only (800) 243-5644 / FAX (505) 988-1025
www.sunstonepress.com

For my Father, George, Mildred, Great Spirit, Feather, Eagle, and Sky. And to my Guardian Angel and Soul Sister, Erwan.

Secret knowledge is what you discover for yourself, when you do the work. When secrets are kept they accumulate power, and when divulged, they lose power. Only should you reveal secrets if you are a teacher.
—Sumiruna

Gracias Señora

The HOLY runs through the grass, the flowers, the wind,
through the canyons, in the quiet and the water.

Stillness
Quietness
Reveal
Reframe
Clarity
Center
Falcon
No searching
Exquisite emptiness
Here
Elaborate
Extravagant
Galaxies
Gold
Artistry
Beauty
The presence
Gratitude
Pouring waterfalls
Amethyst eyelashes
Open eye
Diamond abundance
Precise
Grand intelligence
Dirt
River
Stone
No coverings
Illuminating
Infinite love
Sweet existence
Inner listening
Love affair with the divine.

Hummingbird wingbeat
hovers in silent wonder
acrobatic aerial agility
snatches nectar in midair
with her flower probing beak
Ingesting and releasing
LOVE syrup
Heaven and earth bridge
Flicking her tongue
Into flowers of prayers

Sunrise in the grand cathedral
doors, visions, portals,
mystic play
wake, wake, wake,
deity force, translucent angels, goddess
breath, the Supreme, untouchable, unseen,
seen and touching.

In the forest I bathe with thee;
You crown me with Holy
Hold me in truth
Streams of consciousness
Holy Holy Holy
Purifier
Protector
Goddess of Love
Visions
Serenity
Health
Wealth
Harmony
Inhaling immortality
Holy perfection
I cling to your heavenly armor
Raptured by your glorious light
In your silence a symphony hums
Imprinting cellularly ancient songs
Manifestations dance off my tongue
Arkana of saints angels and guides show me the way
Holy Holy Holy
In the forest exalted and humbled
Cleansing
Washing my spirit — clean
Holy Holy Holy!

Bowing in service is the wings for flight
Something was planted inside of me perhaps many
lifetimes ago and it has been seeding germinating sprouting
and peeking its head out
but now it's full bloom here and happening —
It was a thirty year process that had no other choice left
but to open each precious fold the sweetest petals
lit by the sun
nourished by the rains
and held by the earth
for soooooooooooo long
This isn't just an ordinary bloom as you must know why
— only the ordinary holds the extraordinary — a traveling
of cosmic distance. My petals are burning with beauty
carrying precious dew drops of celestial matter extracted
from traveling far out and deep within.

Love Infusion

Every day
I empty
Self
So I may channel
And let the light pour
Through me
A grace that fills me
A luminating physical
Soul
journey
Voyaging
Traveling
Deeper into the earth
Tasting each drop
A light that permeates everything
Marvelous clean and clear taste
That sits on my lips
A kiss
From GOD
We kiss
The sweetness
A reminder of how thin the veil is between
this world and the next.
Every moment is a mystical discourse
And all I have to do...
BE, LISTEN, FEEL, and SEE.
May your whole being be filled with love

Gratitude is the floor
that gives wings to the sky.
Sipping tea at the Goddess table.
Love is the guest.

Let your hair down
Let the wind blow through you
Let the sun warm you
Open your heart
Let the flowers, trees,
and plants,
Kiss you
Receive the blessings
Breathe in all the gifts
Change your mind
Change your mind
Change your mind
Show your gratefulness
Open your arms
Rise in happiness
Embrace life
Hug the moments
Open and bloom in Love
Live now
It's not a secret, it's just mystery

Solar
Cosmic
Electric
Radiant
Life-giving
SUN
Spirit-food
Medicine
Meditation
Vision
Gazer
Ruby
Violet
Saffron
Citrine
Hues
Riding the ether
Speed of Light
LOVE Frequency
Gold rays
SHINE
Onto
Into
Physical
Psychological
Emotional
Spiritual
Excellence
Invoke
Merge
Balancing
HEALING
Sun Goddess Physician
Vitality
Radiance
Celebrate
JOY
Presence
LIFE!

Love is the door
Love is the floor
Love is the roof
Love is the center

I have such long conversations with the wind.

Love meditation
Under the sacred trees
A transparent sky
Grounded bodies
eye tranced
Locked in loves embrace
They meditate
Wings in flight
To the Divine

Stay with those that know pure love.

Whirling
Whirling
Whirling—Lovers
Twirling
Twirling
Twirling—Light
Spinning
Spinning
Spinning—Angels

Turning
Turning
Turning—Galaxies
Orbiting
Orbiting
Orbiting—Planets
Ecstasy
Ecstatic
Union—Universe
Strings
Songs
Drums—Mystic
In every breath—GOD
In every heart—LOVE

Love
Love
Love—Religion

Prayer
Prayer
Prayer—Ceremony
Music
Music
Music—Poetry
Drumming
Drumming
Drumming—Creation
Surrendering
Emptying
Opening—Vessel
Reed
Flute
Instrument—Breath

Harmony
Melody
Spirit—Sufi
In
With
Towards—GOD
Sacred Center
Palpable Stillness
Lover and Beloved
Cosmic Dimensions
Be still the center is you

She sings hummingbird notes
High notes
Heart notes
Whispering prayers
Colorless wings
Sweet fluid freedom
Light notes
Echoing off the mountaintops
Cascading waterfalls
Spinning notes
Vanishing into the bluest sky
Notes of pure love.

What if we were all prayer flags blowing in the wind.

The weeds are deep and tough
kneeling bending pulling
in the form of a prayer
one by one
hundreds by hundreds
clearing the obstacles
smothering the light
The path always has weeds
trying to prevent you
just keep moving
barefoot and barehanded
You will dance and celebrate with the flowers.

You want it too much, so it doesn't come.
You seek outside, what's already within you.
You try to understand, when it's all clear.
You ask endless questions, instead of listening.
You sniff, instead of smell. You taste, instead of eat.
You peck, nibble, yet never French kiss.
You touch, masturbate, yet never have the orgasms.
You exist, but you never live.
You want love, and it's all around you.
Frustrated and busy, you never pause to smell the
intoxicating fragrance of life.

Softening
Illuminating
Untangling
Lightening
Humming
Coloring
Shooting Arrows
Sacred galaxy
Sun
Moon
Planets
Earth
Trillions of stars
Mother
Father
Great Milky Way
Billions
Trillions
Atoms
Endless space
Sacred Being-ness
Infinite LOVE
Being
Intelligence
Sacred Mind
Birthing rebirthing
Dying
Zero
Master
Growing
Wind
Breath
Dusty
Space
YOU
Sacred Being
Perfect Love
Complete Forgiveness
Experiencing the Intimate

In her wildness I find Soul
Lucious green brilliance
I find Truth
I feel LOVE
Cosmic Laughter
Exotic birds
Teachers that flutter and serenade messages from angels.
Branches like arms that gift me flowers, temple like galaxies releasing pheromones that seduce. Sachamama, mother of the forest, is alive and deeply intelligent, she communicates, interacts, plays, and in high volume! She captivates intrigues softens and humbles. Her quietness invades me...her sublime stillness disciplines me. Her unfathomable wisdom coaches me. She takes me away, calls me to REAL.

Sing
Dance
Pray
Meditate
Drum
Dream
Vision
Intuit
Transform
Transmute
Go deep within
Challenge
Open the doors
Release
Let go
Break free
Rebel
Explore
Stretch and expand
Depths
Heights
Limberness
Inner tides
Flowing
Cuming
Climax
Fullness of light

Eagle flying HIGH with the MOST HIGH
YAHWEH
YESHUA
Soaring Gold White Black Eagle
Amplified by the HOLY SPIRIT
Seraphs and Cherubs
Heavenly realms
Michael the archangel
Pierces through the darkness
LIGHT is the Way
HIGH
HIGH
HIGH
With the ONE
NOBILITY
POWER
BEAUTY
GRACE
FREEDOM
LOVE
Soaring in the SKY with SKY and FEATHER
The HIGHEST HIGH
Pureness
Goodness
Humility
Gratitude
FAITH
AWE
PEACE
HALLELUJAH HALLELUJAH HALLELUJAH

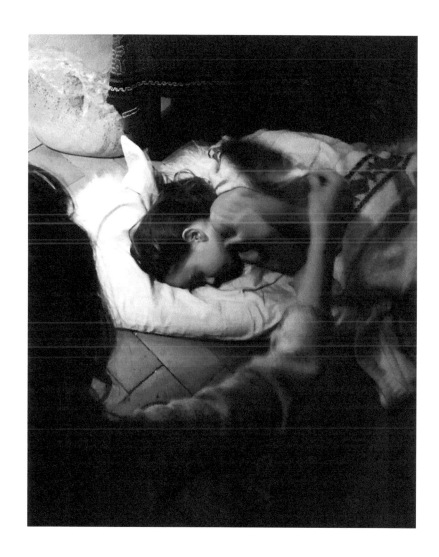

In the dark quietness we sleep
Angels camp all around us
Wings of love
Sweet dreams come in and out
Jasmine and honeysuckle into the crystal
Cave of my heart retrieving ancients messages
Lifetimes of love-
Waking body
Lit by the sun
Imprinting songs of gratitude

Tears...like pearls dropping

Let us plant seeds of Sacred
Every piece of this life is the dance
of ecstasy and madness,
humility and sadness,
and with it ALL—
give thanks.

Love is water
Love is flowers
Love is the blue sky
Love is the storm
Love is the birdsong
Love is the breeze
Love is the trees
Love is the earth
Love is a smile
Love is breath
Love is sunshine
Love is now
Love is grace—gracing you, me, and everyone, every
single day. Giving thanks is the foundation of love.
Prayers of gratitude humble, and give more than we could ever hope for,
Sending love to others is more powerful than you can imagine, sending love
to those who are suffering, or who have hurt you, sending love out to the
world, giving thanks for Mother Earth puts you in the flow of the Cosmos.

Divine union of beauty.
Pacha Mama
Madrecita
Madre Tierra
Madre Vieja
Madre Santa
Senora
Mother Earth
We are made of water, rivers, stones,
forest, plants, flowers, and dirt.
We are the songs of hummingbirds,
the iridescent magic of butterflies,
we are the cosmos.
Like silk you are as beautiful as Mother Earth.
Gracias por esta session.

Sometimes the greatest acts are just showing up.

The Universe has given everything, and we must tune in for this information which is already deep within your cellular DNA. We are in constant flux just as the moon is and we are emanating the celestial bodies of this universe. The moon sets deeply into the ocean just as we descend into the depths of the earth we die and rise again, Mother Earth we are connected to through the navel of our very bodies we are tied drinking her potent herbs and walking barefoot reminds us that we are all native beings, there is an electromagnetic influence from our great cosmic mother that directly balances our whole body the water, earth, fire, and sky and when we live closer to the natural world we can connect profoundly with not only our scared moon cycles, the divine feminine, but with our emotions, attitudes, and our very actions. We co-design our destiny. The earth represent the umbilical cord that binds you to the sun, moon, stars, plants, water, animals, and earth are the instruments for our transformation, apprenticeship and path to mastery. And you are SACRED!

Everything is music. The sounds we can't hear, this show is the sound of Spirit. The planets, stars, comets, supernovas, the morning sunrise painting the sky into a Divine choir. Angelic sounds, heavenly music of creation

Flaming Venus
Uranus
Jupiter and Mars conjunction
Skygazer
Stardawn
Capricorn lovers
Volcanic eruptions
Scattering
Particles
Ashes of light
Stardust
Heralding
Blue SUPERMOON
Blood orange
Total
Lunar ECLIPSE
Sun rising
Sun setting
Take it In
Breathe it out

The light of the stars danced along my naked body floating drifting dreaming
in hot pools of sacred water deep in the Rio Grande extraterrestrial crafts shot
all across the night's sky worlds galaxies comets celestial beings ancestors star
runners star dancers spirits guardians telling stories of past present and future
Venus
Jupiter
Mars
Ceres
Chiron
The Milky Way making brilliant music playing games
A fiesta of goddesses dancing charming the waning half moon
Aquarius Orion Saturn rings of irresistible immaculate charm grace and beauty
heavenly bodies of infinite radiant light door ways nuclear particles atoms of
unknown dimensions...
all in one night soaking in Awe!

Watermelon dripping down my mouth
above Orion's Belt singing ancient songs
with the three sisters / mintaka swallowed up
by two hundred billion stars clustered together
one orgasmic cosmic ejaculation
the Milky Way
soaking in hot champagne waters
jumping in the Rio Grande to cool off
Big horned sheep
tobacco offered to the spirits
mother of waters floating in prayers
sacred quietness
walking the beauty way

Love is water
Will we not thirstily devour that last drop of light,
we were not together yesterday,
but tomorrow will we be lovers?!
Bathe in the waters of your beauty...
because your worth is it.

Water your love. Love is water and we cannot live without either. Love is not knowledge, but wisdom. We need love the moment we are born until we die. Without love you can have righteousness, but righteousness without love is mere arrogance. Pride without love always corrupts, regardless of who you are. You do things you should not do believing you are above others, that no one can teach you anything. Love is service to all the world. Love is all around you. The natural world teaches us the meaning of love. The rocks and trees, the life giving rains, juicy plants, cosmic particles that formed the fabric of life, the great feminine sweetness that when connected with keeps us in a space of beauty, harmony, and love. So many today are angry, bitter, hard, and disconnected completely from Mother Earth, the absence of beauty. Water is the fountain of life, the first medicine, and it purifies, renews, revitalizes, and transforms us. Water yourself regularly and let this love flow all over you, and through you. Get outside alone, with your family, or friends and outstretched arms to the sublime love that is everywhere. The sunrise and sunset, the nightfall rising the moon, the forest and animals, swimming in the sea, soaking in the springs, cold water immersing, sitting under a tree, all of this is so you can evolve, flourish, and walk lightly on this earth.

In stillness the light emanates

Breath is Prayer

The darkness illuminates the light

Solstice
Darkness
Light
Death
Rebirth
Venus
Vega
Philosophers
Sages
Mystics
Seers
Galileo
Jupiter
Orion
Atlantis
Undreamed
Dreamed
Myth
Stories
Night
Morning
Songs
Prayers
Books
Candle
Celebration
Sol
Sun
Standing Still
Maps
Stars
Astrologers
Bethlehem
Jesus
Consciousness
BC
AD

Arabs
Babylonians
Kings
Mother Mary
Conception
Womb
Enlightenment
Death
Life
Babies
Virgo
Mercury
Jupiter
Saturn
Conjunction
Milky Way
Love
Hate
Sinners
Saints
Stonehenge
Ancient ancestors
Christmas
Yule
Deer Dance
Star Runners
Druids
Anastasia
Saturnalia
Wealth
Incandescent
plasma
Winds
Fires
Pine
Cedar
Piñon

Kivas
Smoke
Rooftops
Midnight sky
Fairies
Angels
Michael
Rhythms
Cycles
Frozen
Sacred
Immovable
Call out my name
The star you see
Seasons
Nomadic
Wine
Water
Food
Cloves
Oranges
Spices
Frankincense and
Myrrh
Baptism
Alignment
Superstition
Gods
Masters
Agriculture
Plentiful
Romans
Rational
Scientific
Spiritual
Dances
Ceremonies

Nature
Ice
Quiet
Stillness
Animals
Livestock
Twilight
Plants
Seeds
Flowers
Fragrance
Red
Purple
Royalty
Scribes and
Pharisees
Awareness
Illumination
Dark night
Birthing
Dawn
Calling in
Called out
December
Sun
Welcomes
Capricorn
Stars born

Mother of waters float like moon calling us to our emotional body self, the nurturer, the great feminine power of intuition creativity, patience, compassion and love. All of creation, the earth emerged from the oceans and we have emerged from the amniotic fluid her womb we are born. The full moon is a great time to go deep within and nurture yourself with a floral baths, nourishing perfumes, healing salts, balms, fragrant scents that penetrate your skin and your mind tuning you into the depths of the great feminine force. The moon, stars, and planets are as mysterious, vast, and cosmic as woman, float in the deep waters of your magic and feel the vibration of the cosmos bringing new life and new energy to you, the celestial holy bodies created this dwelling place for you, the magical planet spinning in infinite space to shine and to radiate an aura as majestic as the super moon. We should always take good care of our skin it's where our luminous nature resides. Illuminating All!

Clarity
clairvoyance
How do you SEE, what do you SEE?
vertex planes dimensions
Polish your rings
lucidity
Sharpen your wits
Clear mind
Diamond Radiance -
shiny mind, shiny heart, shiny body.
Bright
Brilliant
Radiant
No negativity, only beauty.
Light
Luminous
Luminaries
fractals crystals galaxies
Polish your rings.
Polish your rings.
Polish your rings.

Feather
Eagle
Sky
Water
Earth
Fire
Cosmic dimension
Be still the center is me
Floating in a prayer of pure love

Pollen Kisses
Her flower opened in full bloom
ripe, fertile, soft and juicy.
Her lips moist, warm, swelling and dripping.
His tongue entered, a mouthful of pollen.

Depth
elevation cosmic dimensions
slithering in the underworld
Yacumama
the great anaconda
creeping the unseen
rising heat
fire and water
dark
fertile
moist
earth
shedding
transforming
DNA
cellular recalibrating
roots
fungi
plants
Vine
flower
swamp
purging
for you
healing
spark spark spark
puff puff puff
high speed
electric vibrations
dark shadows
melting
I see you
sprouting new thoughts
releasing
spinning webs
silk
music
new songs
serpent head peaking
blossoming flower
do you see me?
green earth
I am all of you

Center
Body
Mind
Spirit
Eye
Intelligence
See
Wisdom
Gold
Stardust
Minerals
Metals
Plants
Animals
Shapeshifter
Energy
Whirlpool
Feline
Senses
Geometry
Sacred
Celestial
Radiates
Physical
Matter
Spheres
Light
Dark
Hope
Love
Holiness
Cleanliness
Shiny
No longer

Earthbound
Stardancer
Galaxies
Cells
Dimensions
Forming
Waterfalls
Rivers
Plants
Forests
Sounds
Vibration
Peace
Visions
Rainbows
Limbs
Bodies
Circles
Life
Compassion
Uplifting
Stones
Comets
Mirror
Reflect
Speak
Communication
Currents
Harmonic
Points
Heart
Nature
Humanity
Soar

Inside my visions, my favorite place to be.

The Heavens
The Universe
The Divine
SumiRumi
Señora
Mother
Gracias
PachaMama
Merci
Namaste
Cuz You Slay
You
Noble
Regal
Ayari Wamri
Queen
Seer
Sage
Shaman
Aya
Cosmic serpent
chakruna
Vine
Plants
Ceremony
Dream
See
Visions
Create
Become
BE
Jessika...ka!
One ness
Transformer
Red-tail hawk,
hummingbird,
deer-heart
Sky dancer
Kung foo

Yanapuma
Black panther
Black as the night
Fierce
Hunter
Darkness
Gratitude
Light
Joy
Juice
Active force
Holy Spirit
Orgasm
LOVE
Ecstasy
Bliss
Dance
Songs
Visions
Insights
Downloads
Births
Rubies
Violet
Lapis
Saffron
Diamond
Wisdoms
Hot
Wet and dripping
Liquid Kisses
Lips
Tasting
Drinking
Swallowing
Sweet sweet sweet,
Delicious soup
Celestial prayers
Extraterrestrial

Starships
Portals
Past
Present
Future
Secrets
Whispers on the
wind
Foot tracks pass by
the horizon
Sage
Sand
Pearls
Revelations
Constellations
Watery Supermoon
wondrous rising
Deity
Moonbows
Rainbows
Yakumama
slithering
Moon bathing
Stretching
Moving
Twisting
Sliding all around
the water
With her tail
In
and
Out
Like a big tongue
Drinking from the
life flow,
Amerita
Drink me, swallow
me
Yakumama

Yanapuma
Red tail hawk
Eagle
Galaxies in galaxies
Traveling starlight
Bubbling
Champagne
Lucious
Cosmic honey
Arkanas
Icaros
Blessings
Prayers
Songs
Moans
Silence...Meditation
Drums
Hums The Universe
The Divine
The Sacred
Calls out to me
Out of my mouth
Evoking
Saying
Spelling
speaking
Singing
Clairvoyant
Psyche
Vegetalista
Flying saucers
Angels
Comets
Cancer Supermoon
conjunction
Kayadeeeedee

Fast from the mind.
Fast from people.
Fast from materialism.
Fast from noise.
Fast from food.
Fast into silence
and cultivate patience.

Holy
quiet
moments
electric vibrations
beautiful, soulful, strength of mystery.
Wild, humbling, exhilarating, and exalting.
Every taste, color, and fragrance...love
medicine.

Guardians of Mother Earth
Smoking her pipe
Intense heat and fire
In the earth
Because it is her domain
Extrasensory dimensions
Traveling to unknown realms
Consume combustible materials
Alchemical fires
Eruption
She is all elemental
A diva
Connoisseur
Red
Warms her
The red aura
Spiritual energy
Journeying through other worlds
In one sunrise
Bonded in the heart of earth
Snake coiled around the universe.

Soul and joy of a child
Relentless warrior of love
Holy
Cosmic
Architecture
Glorious beautiful opera
Extracted unfolded
Seeding planting germinating
Attainable source of all Beingness
Songs carried to the most sensitive parts of me...
kayadeeedee!
Scrubbing me raw
Opening eyes
And doors
Love evoking visions
Schooling
Transporting
Grounding
Beautiful journey
Attentive apprentice
Symbolic deaths
Direct
Intense
Dense
Content
Shaping
Forming
Guiding
Wise
Gentle
Humorous
Artist
Purifying lifting my heart

SunseX

Red earth
Scattered
Winds of time
Before her it is beautiful
Navajo song-prayer
Ancient Mud castles
Stupendous failures
Movement
Footprints
Desert silence
Running
Faraway beauty
Risky moves
Building the invisible
Stories
Visions
Storytelling
Calling in the visible
Success applauded
Dreams paint into the landscape
Spark of fire
Burns
No borders
Breathing globe
Life well lived
Quietness
Spirit
Physical form
Opinions
Independent free spirit
Private dialogue the Universe
Pottery canvas
Obstacles
Laughing girl
Pursuits of her vision
Runner

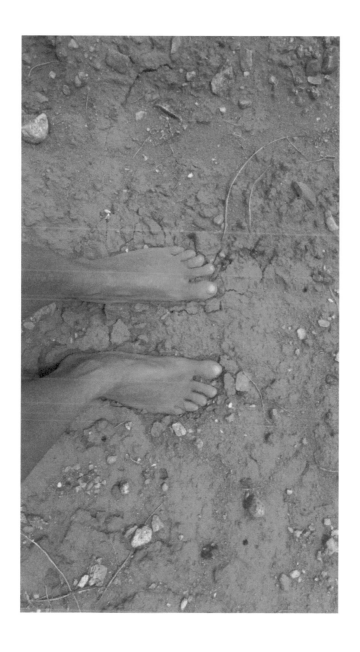

Snow dusted
Piñon over the foothills
Sun sanctuary
Pueblo prayers
Sacred mountain
Truchas Peak and Cerro Perdernal
Talk to each other
She sun-gazes
She bows
She sits
Breathing
Silent
AWE
Rainbow Kachina dancers
Departing spirits
White light
Interpretations
Sprinkle on the black oak trees
Precious secret
Dried goldenrod
Water
Sage
Juniper
O'Keeffe
Mabel
Tony
D.H. Lawrence
Crumbled adobe walls
Wild rough land
It will either hold you
Or
Spit you out
Healers
Travelers
Sharp flint
Cold moist ground
She sits tall on her rock
Quietness warms her like a blanket
Sunset

She moves me
She fills me up
She pulls me in
She pulls me out
She holds me
She is the solid earth
On which I move

Clear your head, clear the mind, walk, hike, run, feel the quiet, smell the cow dung, feel the cold wind blowing against your face, sit under an old juniper tree, watch the antelope, talk with the crows, feel the sky, hop a fence, fucks trails, get cold, get hot, feel uncomfortable, feel yourself and nature and nothing else.

Silence so much more beautiful than words
Silence the poem.

Rider on the storm
Centered
Fierce
I shoot arrows of beauty
I move stealth like a deer
I gather ammo from flowers
Water Spirits
Trees
Butterflies
Sage
Yarrow
Nettle
Hawks pass me secrets on the wind
I dance on my Eagle in a circling Galaxy
dropping rings of Milky Way love on my
enemies.

This now, will never be better. This is the gift. The now. The sun against my naked body, the sparkling blue sky, the water rambling, and the earth that holds me. The tears that flow from my eyes in gratitude of all this NOW. It's so simple, but it's not...when you fully understand the magnitude of living—that every second is gold, a grand humility washes over you and every single thing you do becomes prayer.

Running
Leaping
A gazelle in flight
Pollen
Wind
Flowers
Sweat
Barefoot
Sage
Indian paintbrush
Cactus
Flint
Obsidian shards
Dust
Heart drumming
Whispers of my ancestors
Prayer
Breath
Fire
Peace
Solitude
Endless space
Activated
Strengthened
Humbled
Grounded
Spirit work
Dissolving into the sky

Piñon burns sweet somatic earth
twirling whispering releasing
ancient mud walls—
Deep aquifers veins of medicine water—
floating floating floating
Stillness penetrates every cell
Love consumes every breath
Silence my dearest friend—
Mica shimmers from cliffs made of sand
I hear the songs, I hear them
water and fire high prayers
listen listen listen
and the night sky a remembrance of the star
people and the reminder of their presence.

I follow the wild tracks
down and up
over the mountains
and to the top
sometimes I look back
feeling far out the distance
smiling a stare
a quiet reflection
of times passed
and I stand looking down
at my feet and legs
the dirt and scratches
But then I turn my face up
and toward the sun
and I smile
sometimes a tear drops
and I ponder all that my eyes
have seen
all that my heart has felt
all that's scattered in the wind
all that's left to come
I never regret
I am so grateful for all the presents
The red tail hawk a flamboyant fierce
messenger
and the desert flowers
that soften the path
the elk that move
steady and stealth
fertilizing the earth
Juniper brushing my shoulders
Cedar in my hair
Cactus that sometimes
make me bleed
Arrowheads lifting from arroyo beds
ancestors nudging me along in spirit
Antlers in my hands
like a warrior shield
And the next mountains
the cool streams
the sweet flowers
and the sun that sits content

Ink blotches freckled the dark far sky
faint sounds came in and out
sudden rapid winds blew rain, then snow
they appeared, bird migration
dancing like ballerinas
winged songs moving north
the sun broke, the oak shimmered
and I plunged in the last of winters
cold water

People love to talk, people thrive on it, they gossip, slander, initiate, ignite, seed, plant, water...negativity! Minds and hearts wounded, jaded, full of anger, resentment, pain, hatred, envy, jealousy, insecurities, and smallness. Few...grasp, reach, dig, claw, climb for goodness, for light, for love. It's easier to stay in the stinky swamp, stuck in the wounds of the past, easier to play the victim, the victim after all knows that role well, plays that role well, has gotten by...barely, being the victim, after all the victim role gets sympathy...oh poor you...it's okay...it's not your fault... this is just what life handed you. Right. Right?! Maybe. Life is hard... right. Neglect, abandonment, abuse, drugs, manipulation, violence, mind control, circumstances that no one should have to experience, levels of evil that are unfathomable. Takes so much to just to feel good, even for a moment...for many. I know. I write this knowing, knowing intimately the pain many feel. I've witnessed it, closely. Thank goodness for the balance, the balance of both. For people who really are happy, because they somehow shine a great light on the beauty that is all around us. Thank god for the poets, the artists, musicians, the light bearers that get up and do what needs to be done every day...to stir something soft and shiny inside each of us, thank god for those that love, and love well. Thank god for those despite the pain that rise and keep rising to bring in a new day...a new way of seeing...a new way of being...a new way of loving. Thank god for the sunrise, the sunset, the exquisite birdsong that lifts and twists your spirit up into the sky. Thank god for the rivers, the forests, the sacred union of man and women that creates life, for the children whose laughter that brings back the soul. Thank god for this cosmic universe of sublime origins that refreshes, cleanses, and transforms us, invites us, calls us again and again, for every stone, luscious plant, to attend the fragrant flower of life.

The sweetness of a daffodil
Transported me
Her hypnotic notes still lingers on my nose
Her euphoric aroma dazzles in my mind
Breathing in light
Wave after wave her cosmic odor
Wafting through every fold of me
Penetrating my very soul
I breathed her in so deeply
We became one form
White soft delicious petals
Enchanting sweetness
Yellow cheery laughter silky drippings of honey spice
Chantilly cream dancing in your dreams
Vanilla pollen jasmine kisses
Leaving lips wet with nectar

Plants are the vehicle of all life. The Breath, the active force, the heart space. Deep connection with Mother Earth opens our hearts our longing and union with the natural world is some romantic idea, the pain we experience when we seen the natural world being destroyed affects our hearts, we feel betrayal and it directly cause heart break. Spend time outside communicating with the plants draws us closer and helps deepen our appreciation restoring joy to our hearts, healing takes place cellularly, breathing new life and enabling more room for love.

Sunset eruption
Peony high priestess
Violet metaphysician magic maker
wrapped with the sunset matching her soul
Yarrow streaming consciousness
Blazing flames of beauty
Sunflower enlightenment
And she wore the sunset like a crown tonight
Rose opening the heart
Lavender clean
Poppy high
Wild beauty

She greets me with hollyhocks
petal kisses
exchanges of sacred medicine
In the car down the old old dirt road
conversations constellations
bounce off her hair
antennas
sweetgrass
maze
sunrise moon
monsoons
hummingbirds
echoes in the canyon
collect the grain
sunshine in the rain
deer medicine at our feet
we run for lilies
memories of lifetimes
in the thick mauve thistles
my relationship with you.

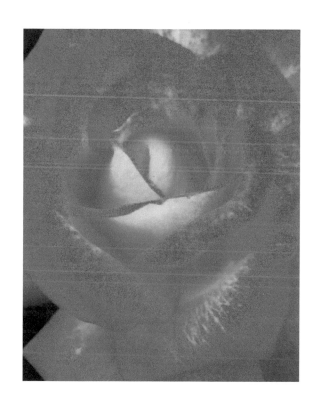

They say a person's eyes are the window or the mirror of the soul. They can reflect wisdom and compassion. They're spiritual pathways. Behind my eyes are tunnels, worlds, galaxies, constellations, kaleidoscope of sapphire multifaceted rainbows, Cherokee Stars, emanations, and brilliant multifaceted waves of LOVE.

A daffodil that still lingers on my mind, something like a lover far away, yet so close to you...lost in fragrance. For a moment she was the center of my universe, I wanted to explore every fold, crevice, and inch of her, the way you do with a lover. She was intoxicating, delightful, mesmerizing, silky sweet goodness. She called me, invited me in, among the glorious gladiolus and raving freesia, she with her wafting mysterious enchanting perfume...among the tall grass. A daffodil.

Fleeting
Swirling
Flames
Cosmic
Gold
flakes
Glitter
Sparrow hawk
Rainbows
Thunder
Deer
Rain
Leaves
Sap
Vanilla
Cedar
Drops
Dropping
Sunsets
Osmosis
Morph
Locked
Sacred
Falling
Falling

For you I'd be a sunflower do you hear my enlightening laughter?

I'm just a bird singing my songs—

Once upon a time a little girl believed that if she loved pure enough, if she honored all of nature, if she hiked every mountain, swam in all the seas, smelled every flower, gave thanks for every drop, listened to every stone, blew with every wind, danced with every thunder, laughed with every tree, played with every animal, woke with every sunrise, gave thanks for every sunset, humbled like the fallen leaves, spoke with every plant—somehow and someway her songs would be heard . May our lives show more than our words. Some of the greatest acts are just showing up. That little girl was watching she was the lead character, and she created despite the dark, the hurts, and all the tears a life that participated with beauty. Every time she fell, she got right back up, the cold got warmer, the pine needles stopped poking, the altitude got higher, and she flew high above the clouds on the wings of love.

In the green pasture we walked
hand n' hand, bare feet, big feet, little feet,
Giggling our way to the yurt.
dandelion, red clover, moon flowers,
popping, opening, under the bright sapphire sky.
Black, pink, and red hollyhocks, tall sunflowers,
white and purple iris
swaying, waving, smiling,
in the evening july breeze
southeast high peaks, white icing
left from winter, and the acequia flowing
strong. O mother of pearl majesty rises, centering,
lucid rings of milky ancient light.
Little hands open the small painted wooden yurt door,
One by one, cozy and snuggled to each other,
padded beds on the floor
we sleep.
A light in the center fills the room through a glass sky,
thunder plowing the earth, rushing rain, drumming love songs.
Midnight, Lover whispers come outside with me...stealth like
Eagles away from the nest, hunting magic unexpected prisms
Moonbow
Moonbow
Moonbow
a rainbow on a moonlit ride!

About the Author

"No Method, No Teacher, No Guru."
—Van Morrison

I grew up in a small village in southern New Mexico called Cloudcroft, a pasture for the clouds. It had a population of less than four hundred at that time. Despite being known as an arid region it stands as one of the highest villages in the United States. My parents are George and Georgia and my two older brothers Zach and Justin. Cloudcroft is high altitude country in a desert sky high oasis, hence the name. My grandparents were well known in those parts and helped build the rail line that would bring in many loggers to create this magic spot. My granddad was a banker, a brilliant man who helped build the high rolls tunnel. My family also owned at one time the historic Lodge, a beautiful castle-like resort built in 1899.

My granddad met my grandmother while logging for timber. He saw her soaking in the river in Box Canyon and fell in love with her. He proposed that very day and my grandma said yes but not until she finished college, which she did at the United World College in Las Vegas in northern New Mexico five years later. She was a spitfire who would walk across the trestles fifty-two feet high or more on stilts for money. My dad agreed and said she was fearless.

The Cloudcroft area was valuable in forming my younger years. It was an unbelievable expanse filled with forest, rivers, meadows, and fields of endless wild flowers. It was in this sky house that I could dream, write, play, run, harvest plants, and watch the stars that gave me the tools I would need to be strong, wild, and free.

My parents have now been married for almost fifty years and are two of my favorite people. I am truly grateful for both of them. They are complete opposites—my mother extremely religious and my father a very spiritual free thinker and nature man. This duality helped shape and form my very being. From a young girl I beat my own drum. I was always rebellious, meaning I didn't like to conform to anyone else's views. I didn't like being told what the world was or what I should believe or think. Rather, I needed to experience my own spirituality my own way. This wasn't easy. My mom was very set in her ways and believed them to be the only true way.

I attended her meetings three times a week, gave talks, and even went to other countries to preach and tell of the good news and the end of this world. I read the Bible daily and I have read it six times in its entirety. But it wasn't for me, and I struggled. I knew very young that I was seeing, feeling, and experiencing life differently. You could take me to all the sermons you want, study the Bible, study yoga, study the dharma, but I knew god was in the riverbank, in the woods, in the flowers, rambling in the waters, whispering in the grass, shooting across the sky, blowing in the wind– consciousness was everywhere and flowing through me. I found god under the dark night sky while talking to the moon. I AM. I am not a sheep nor is anyone my shepherd. Religion as I came to know it seemed a sham, a business, a way to keep the collective conditioned to whatever the belief is. Heaven and hell is every day; you make it so by what you choose to believe, how you love, the way you perceive.

Love only this group
all others are blind,
believe only this truth,
all others are lost.

I was never interested in being told "the way it is." Buddha, Jesus, Muslim, Hindu, Jew, Catholic, Baptist, Sikh...it's all the same to me, a practice of following someone who is believed to have been enlightened or the son of god, yet also an adherence and obedience to a way, the way, that is right, that will give you the truth to become holy, clean, free, and enlightened. Except no one in these sects or groups has yet to become the next enlightened, the next prophet, or the next guru only because they were right.

This is nonsense to me and always has been. Consciousness is everywhere in everything and I am. I am enlightened, I am awake, I am awake to the blind leading the blind. I don't have a teaching to share, but rather an awake fullness that is burning inside me. I am happy because I am free. I am radiant and shiny because I live without anyone telling me how. I attend the grand cathedral that is spinning in a universe of unfathomable magic. To pretend I know it all or I have found the truth would be a lie. And yet I have experienced GOD in silence, in aloneness, in prayer, in nature, and in love—a bright cosmic knowing that leads me over and over again to this nowness, this precious infinite nowness that keeps transforming and dissolving into the sky. I need no temple, church, priest, teacher, or place to experience Source. I open my eyes or close them, sitting or lying down, running or skipping, laughing or crying, arms full of love, or hands empty. I am one with it all.

My very faith is as solid as the ground I stand on, and as ungrounded as a bird in flight. I'm not interested in solving the mystery. I'm not interested in a god that separates people good from bad, heaven or hell. I'm not interested in being led. I don't pay to have my sins forgiven, nor do I need an intermediary to talk to god. I don't need to sit, chant, repeat mantra after mantra or breathe in some ancient method to feel my kundalini rising. My crown chakra is beaming, glowing, radiant light. I don't need a shaman when the maestra is the plants, Mother Earth, I am god and god is me. Each morning I wake in perfect love and gratitude, in every direction a kiss from the divine. As far as the east is to the west I am blessed. It's in the smile and laughter of my kids, the morning coffee, the land that greets me, orgasms, the sunrise and sunset painting the sky. I don't need clothes to cover my gorgeous healthy body, or to make you happy. I don't need a title or anyone's name to drop to feel like I am somebody. I am everything and everything is me. I dance in all circles and in none.

I'm the "it" you wannabe
I've seen you jump on my
bandwagon
Tryin' to keep up with my speed
I'm fast and ferocious
cuz I lead
You're slow and furious

cuz you follow
Ya I channel with the great
Cosmic Sufi Rumi Sagan Cherokee Star Blackfoot brilliance
I'm talkin' Quechua Shipibo my own medicine Icaros sweat lodge Van
Morrison wavelength genius
Hendrix and Led Zeppelin leavin' you spinnnnning
Kick you in the face Billy Jack
half breed
Paul Newman and Redford
THE BIG STING
Blowing a mirage in the wind
You desperately trying to grab
Coyote trickster shape shifter
Divin' off the precipice
Soaring with my eagle wings
Copal in your face
Ya smudge yourself cuz you need the help...authentic? You don't even
know what that means
You've got all the accessories of the costume, good job!
Artifices are for those who try, hard, hard, hard
Georgia O'Keeffe "don't even sign my paintings cuz I know who I am"
Jim Morrison break on through to the other side and some frijole beans ha
ha ha...Did you see your name on the list? Nah cuz you're not even in the
league—
Oh and that's my ass—kiss it.

My father would take me hiking for whole days and we would spread
out. Eventually meeting along the way, we'd sit under the stars with his
telescope watching shooting stars. We'd pick raspberries in the patches
among bears. I'd climb trees perched with hawks and eagles and sit on
top of mountains in complete silence watching the sunset. I'd eat flowers,
talk with birds, hunt, and run miles, sing and dance while my dad played
guitar, read poetry, philosophy, science, and write while sitting under giant
ponderosas. This was freedom, and this is where I tuned in and would call
in all the questions, answers blowing in the wind.

I eventually knew I could not be a part of any organized system that believed it had the truth. This was just a long beginning of awakening, and remembering. I knew what I felt in nature to be my truest self. I knew that I was already one with it all, with god. I could look at the moon and the magnificent sky and feel the pull of constellations and galaxies. I knew that whatever I thought I knew was just scratching the surface of a Cosmic Divine energy that was in everything and everyone. I knew that this, this human life, this incredible gift was the gift. Heaven and hell are a state of mind. That the gift was to drink in the moment, all the moments, let the wisdom drop like gold sweet rays of sun shine deep in the eyes of your consciousness. My childhood freedom of open space allowed this expansive self to be.

I apprenticed with plant teachers for over ten years. I've traveled all over the world. I sit with plants and learn songs, I immerse in the language of life...the plants and all of mother earth is the gift. I immerse in deep being and in plant sutras. I've been a consumer of knowledge and a connoisseur of consciousness. Along the way I married my husband Erwan, my soul sister, we created three diamonds, Feather, Eagle, and Sky. I created my whole plant medicine skin care line after their names. We travel all over the world, holding ceremony working with plants and tribes.

We live in northern New Mexico in a high mountain village in between Santa Fe and Taos on eleven acres with water running through our land, animals, and the most majestic mountains. This land holds me, a land of rich culture and wild country, over twenty pueblos that still dance and sing, and that still live a traditional native lifestyle. The only way for me to live is in deep connection with the land. It's the oldest way. Hands and feet in the earth, naked in the sunshine, planting, growing, foraging, and hunting our own food, ceremony, song and dance, prayerful being. Rising with the sun, being still...listening. Prayers and tobacco offered. My full attendance to the dance.

Gracias Señor.
Life is the Ceremony.

CPSIA information can be obtained
at www.ICGtesting.com
Printed in the USA
BVHW02n1417081018
529573BV00009B/89/P